Happily Ever After: Using Life Insurance Without Dying

Because Some Things Are Not Worth Dying For

FOR MY FATHER

ISBN: 9798391403456

Table of Contents

Happily Ever After?

Happily Ever After?

Let's face it. Some things are not worth dying for. And a large life insurance payout is not one of them: if you're the insured, I can guarantee you're not seeing a dime of the death benefit. And if you're insuring a loved one, you will certainly find no amount of money will relieve the grief you are feeling and bring them back.

But what if you could use life insurance to live a better life? To not only retire more comfortably, but achieve your dreams?

In this book, you'll read stories about families who did just that. Even confirmed bachelors and bachelorettes who did just that. And along the way come to understand in easy to understand language the technical aspects of life insurance to help you make this difficult decision today.

Written by a real life insurance agent, you'll gain decades of perspective to see why life insurance is very much a tool best used for living by those of us wanting to live fuller, happier lives.

Story Time Examples! (Spoiler Alert: Everyone in These Stories Lives Because No One Wants to Hear ANOTHER Story About Someone Dying to Use Their Life Insurance!)

The Martinez Family Moves Across the Country to A Dream Job with a Universal Life Insurance Policy

Meet the Martinez family: a happy and healthy family of four living in the suburbs, Mr. and Mrs. Martinez and their two young children.

Mr. and Mrs. Martinez have been thinking about the future of their children and their retirement. They know that they need to start planning now to ensure that they are financially secure for the long term. They have been hearing a lot about **universal life insurance** and are considering purchasing a policy.

One of the unique features of universal life insurance is the ability to build cash value over time. This cash value grows tax-deferred, meaning the family does not have to pay taxes on the growth until they withdraw it. The Martinez family saw this as a potential opportunity to grow their savings.

They decided to purchase a universal life insurance policy and set it up so that a portion of their monthly premiums would go towards building cash value. The policy also had a guaranteed minimum interest rate, so they knew that their cash value would always grow at least that much.

Over the years, the cash value in their policy began to grow. They were happy to see their savings increase and knew that they were on the right track towards achieving their financial goals.

One day, Mr. Martinez received an unexpected job offer in another state. The family had to consider the costs of moving and the potential loss of income for Mrs. Martinez during the transition. They also had to think about the impact of the move on their children's education and social life.

Fortunately, the cash value in their universal life insurance policy came in handy. They were able to withdraw some of the cash value to help cover the costs of moving and the potential loss of income. This eased their financial burden and gave them some peace of mind during the transition.

As time passed, the Martinez family continued to grow their cash value. They knew that they could access the cash value at any time for any reason, including paying for their children's education, taking a much-needed vacation, or supplementing their retirement income.

The Martinez family also liked the flexibility of their universal life insurance policy. They could adjust the death benefit as their needs changed. If they wanted to increase their coverage, they could do so without having to apply for a new policy. This meant that they could always have the right amount of coverage for their family's needs.

In addition to the cash value and flexibility, the Martinez family also appreciated the tax benefits of their universal life insurance policy. The death benefit is generally paid out tax-free to beneficiaries, which would provide financial protection for their loved ones if something were to happen to Mr. or Mrs. Martinez.

Overall, the Martinez family was very happy with their universal life insurance policy. They felt that it provided them with the protection they needed and the flexibility they desired. The cash value helped them achieve their financial goals and provided them with a safety net in case of unexpected expenses.

The Li Family Survives Breast Cancer with an Protection Indexed Universal Life Insurance Policy

The Li family consists of Mr. and Mrs. Li and their two children. Both parents work full time and they depend on their income to pay their mortgage, bills, and support their children's education. They also have some savings, but they worry about the future and want to ensure that they have financial security in case anything unexpected happens.

After doing some research, they decide to purchase a **protection indexed universal life insurance** policy. This type of policy provides a death benefit to their beneficiaries in case of the policyholder's death, but it also has additional benefits that can help the policyholders while they are alive.

One of the unique features of this policy is that it has an investment component that is linked to an index, such as the S&P 500. The policyholders can choose to allocate a portion of their premiums to this investment component, which can potentially grow over time. If the index performs well, the policy's cash value can increase, providing a source of savings for the family.

Mr. and Mrs. Li decide to allocate a portion of their premiums to this investment component, as they believe that it can provide a higher return than a traditional savings account. They also like the fact that their cash value will be protected from any potential market losses, as this type of policy has a floor rate that guarantees a minimum return.

In addition to the investment component, this policy also has a rider that can provide living benefits in case of a critical illness, such as cancer or a heart attack. If one of the policyholders is diagnosed with a covered critical illness, they can access a portion of the death benefit while they are alive to help cover medical expenses, pay bills, or make up for lost income due to their illness.

One day, Mrs. Li is diagnosed with breast cancer. She needs to take time off work to undergo treatment and the family's income is reduced. Fortunately, they had purchased the protection indexed universal life insurance policy with the critical illness rider. Mrs. Li is able to access a portion of the death benefit to help cover her medical expenses and make up for lost income while she is undergoing treatment. This provides much-needed financial support for the family during a difficult time.

After Mrs. Li recovers from her illness, the family continues to pay their premiums and allocate a portion to the investment component. Over time, the cash value of their policy grows, providing a source of savings for their future. They also have peace of mind knowing that they have a death benefit that can provide financial support to their beneficiaries in case anything unexpected happens to them.

In conclusion, the Li family's protection indexed universal life insurance policy provides them with financial security and peace of mind. The investment component of the policy allows them to potentially grow their cash value over time, while the critical illness rider provides living benefits in case of a covered illness. This type of policy is a good fit for families like the Li's who want both protection and potential growth for their savings.

The Patels' Repair their Home with an Accumulation Indexed Universal Life Policy

Meet the Patel family - Mr. and Mrs. Patel, and their two young children. The Patels have always been financially savvy, and they understand the importance of saving for their future. However, they want to explore different options to help their money grow faster, while still ensuring that they have access to their savings in case of an emergency. This is where **Accumulation Indexed Universal Life insurance** comes in.

The Patels decide to invest in an Accumulation Indexed Universal Life policy, which offers both a death benefit and a cash value component that can grow tax-free over time. They opt for this policy because they want to accumulate savings for the long-term and take advantage of potential market gains.

The policy offers a variety of investment options, including indexed accounts that allow them to participate in market gains without being exposed to market losses. The Patels choose to allocate a portion of their premium payments to an indexed account that tracks the performance of the S&P 500 Index.

Over time, the value of their cash accumulation account grows as the indexed account performs well. The policy also offers a guaranteed minimum interest rate, so they know their account will never lose value even if the market has a downturn.

One day, the Patels encounter an unexpected financial emergency - their home has a leaky washing machine, and the damage is not covered by their home insurance! And they do not have enough cash saved up to cover the cost. They remember that their Accumulation Indexed Universal Life policy has a feature that allows them to borrow against their cash value account.

They contact their insurance company and request a loan against their cash value account. The insurance company approves the loan, and the Patels receive the funds they need to repair their home. They continue to make premium payments on the policy, and the interest on the loan is added to their cash value account.

As the years go by, the Patels continue to make premium payments and watch their cash value account grow. They also have the option to adjust their premium payments and death benefit as their financial situation changes.

When their children reach college age, the Patels decide to use a portion of their cash value account to pay for their education expenses. They are able to withdraw the funds without penalty, and the money they use for college expenses is tax-free.

Finally, as they near retirement age, the Patels begin to consider their legacy and the impact they want to make on their community. They decide to name their favorite charity as a beneficiary on their Accumulation Indexed Universal Life policy. This ensures that a portion of their wealth will go towards supporting a cause they care about, even after they are gone.

In conclusion, the Patel family's use of an Accumulation Indexed Universal Life policy allowed them to invest in the market while also accumulating savings for the long-term. The policy's cash value component provided them with the flexibility to access their savings in case of an emergency, pay for their children's education expenses, and ultimately leave a legacy to support a cause they care about.

Benjamin Brown, a Bachelor with no Beneficiaries, Uses a Whole Life Policy to Enjoy His Life

Meet Benjamin Brown, a 35-year-old single man with no children, no spouse, and no beneficiaries that would benefit from a life insurance policy. Benjamin is healthy, active, and enjoys his job as an engineer. He has a decent salary and some savings in his bank account. One day, Benjamin hears about whole life insurance from a colleague at work, and he decides to explore the possibility of purchasing a policy for himself.

Benjamin meets with an insurance agent to discuss the details of a whole life policy. The agent explains that whole life insurance is a type of permanent life insurance that provides coverage for a lifetime, as long as the premiums are paid. The agent also explains that whole life policies have a cash value component, which can grow over time and be accessed by the policyholder if needed.

Although Benjamin has no beneficiaries that would benefit from the policy, he realizes that a whole life policy can still benefit him in several ways. First, he can use the cash value component of the policy as a form of savings. The cash value grows over time, and Benjamin can withdraw or borrow against the cash value if needed. This could be useful if Benjamin ever faced an unexpected expense, such as a medical emergency or a car repair.

Second, Benjamin realizes that the cash value component of a whole life policy can also provide him with a source of retirement income. If Benjamin continues to pay his premiums and allows the cash value to grow over time, he could eventually use the cash value as a supplement to his retirement income. This could be especially valuable since Benjamin has no spouse or children to rely on for financial support in his retirement years.

Benjamin decides to purchase a whole life policy with a death benefit that is equal to the amount of his outstanding mortgage. This will ensure that his mortgage will be paid off in the event of his unexpected death. Benjamin also chooses to pay slightly higher premiums to maximize the cash value component of the policy.

Over the next few years, Benjamin pays his premiums on time and watches as the cash value of his policy grows. He does not need to withdraw or borrow against the cash value yet, but he feels secure knowing that the option is available to him if needed. He also feels a sense of relief knowing that his mortgage will be paid off in the event of his unexpected death, even though he has no dependents that would benefit from the policy.

As Benjamin approaches retirement age, he meets with his financial advisor to discuss his retirement income options. His advisor explains that he can start taking withdrawals from the cash value component of his whole life policy to supplement his retirement income. Benjamin decides to take a portion of his retirement income from the policy and the remainder from his other retirement accounts.

Overall, Benjamin is happy with his decision to purchase a whole life policy. Even though he has no dependents that would benefit from the policy, he appreciates the security and flexibility that the policy provides. The cash value component has given him a sense of financial stability, and he knows that the death benefit will help charities he cares about in the event of his death to make the world a better place and establish his legacy.

Why the Kelly Family Chose to Convert their Term Policy

The Kelly family is a young family of four, living in a cozy house in the suburbs. The parents, Tom and Sarah Kelly, are both in their mid-thirties and have two young children, Emily, who is five, and Alex, who is two.

Tom is the sole breadwinner of the family and has his own business, a popular neighborhood pub. Sarah is a stay-at-home mom, taking care of the kids and managing the household. They have a comfortable life, but they are also very conscious about their finances, as they want to ensure that their family is well-provided for in case something unexpected happens.

They have heard about **term life insurance** and are considering getting a policy to protect their family's financial future. They know that term life insurance is a type of life insurance that provides coverage for a set period, usually between 10 and 30 years. They also know that if the policyholder dies within the term, the death benefit will be paid out to the beneficiaries tax-free.

The Kellys decide to meet with a financial advisor to help them determine the right amount of coverage and term length for their needs. After discussing their current income, expenses, and future financial goals, the financial advisor recommends that Tom gets a term life insurance policy with a death benefit of $500,000 for a 20-year term.

Tom and Sarah decide to go ahead with the policy and are relieved to know that if anything were to happen to Tom during the term of the policy, their family would be financially protected. They also understand that the policy would expire at the end of the 20-year term, and if Tom outlives the policy, there would be no payout.

Over the years, Tom and Sarah continue to pay the premiums on the policy, and they feel confident that they have taken an important step in securing their family's financial future. As their children grow older and become more independent, they realize that they may not need as much coverage as they did when they first got the policy.

They decide to meet with their financial advisor again to discuss their options. The advisor explains that they could either let the policy expire at the end of the term or convert it to a permanent life insurance policy.

Tom and Sarah are intrigued by the idea of a permanent policy, which could provide coverage for the rest of Tom's life and offer additional benefits, such as cash value accumulation and the ability to borrow against the policy. However, they are also concerned about the higher premiums that come with a permanent policy.

After carefully considering their options, they decide to convert their term life policy to a permanent policy. They feel that the added benefits and security of a permanent policy are worth the increased cost. They continue to pay the premiums and watch as the cash value of the policy grows over time.

Years later, when Tom and Sarah are in their golden years and have retired, they decide to take advantage of the cash value in the policy. They use it to supplement their retirement income, take a dream vacation, and even help pay for their grandchildren's education.

Overall, the Kelly family was able to use term life insurance to protect their family during their younger years, and then convert it to a permanent policy to provide added security and financial flexibility in their later years

The Abara Family Saves for the Future with a Term Life Insurance Policy

The Abara family has always been good with money. They save a portion of their income every month and invest it in the stock market. John Abara, the father, has been considering getting life insurance for himself for a while now, but he was never sure what type of policy to get. He talked to his friend, who worked as a financial advisor, and he recommended that he get a **term life insurance** policy.

John was hesitant at first, but he did his research and found out that a term life insurance policy is a temporary policy that provides coverage for a specific period, typically 10, 20, or 30 years. He also found out that term life insurance policies have lower premiums compared to whole life insurance policies. This is because whole life insurance policies offer lifetime coverage and build cash value, whereas term life insurance policies only provide coverage for a specific period.

The Abara family decided to purchase a 20-year term life insurance policy for John. The policy provided coverage of $500,000, which would cover their family's needs in case something happened to John during the policy period. The premiums for the policy were relatively low, which allowed the

Abara family to save the difference between the low premium and a higher cost whole life policy.

John continued to save a portion of his income every month and invested it in the stock market. He also made sure to put some money aside for emergencies. John knew that he could invest the money he saved from the low premiums in the stock market, which would give him a higher return than what he would get from a whole life insurance policy. This would allow him to grow his wealth faster and have more money to pass down to his family in case something happened to him.

After the 20-year policy period was up, the Abara family was happy to learn that John was still in good health and did not need to renew the policy. The family was also happy to know that they were able to save a considerable amount of money by opting for a term life insurance policy instead of a whole life insurance policy. They were able to invest the money they saved in the stock market, which allowed them to grow their wealth and have more money for their future needs.

The Abara family's decision to go with a term life insurance policy was a wise one. They were able to get the coverage they needed at a lower premium, which allowed them to save money that they could invest in the stock market. By doing so, they were able to grow their wealth faster and have more money for their future needs. The low premium of the policy allowed the Abara family to enjoy the benefits of having life insurance while still having the flexibility to invest in other areas that would give them a higher return.

Jane Suzuki Preserves Protects Her Fortune

Jane Suzuki was a wealthy retired grandmother who had spent her life building up a sizable fortune for her family. She had raised three children who had all gone on to successful careers, and now she wanted to make sure that her grandchildren and great-grandchildren would be taken care of as well.

One day, Jane met with her financial advisor to discuss her estate planning. Her advisor suggested that she consider purchasing a life insurance policy to help preserve her fortune tax-free for her children upon her death. Jane was intrigued by the idea and asked her advisor to explain how it would work.

The advisor explained that a life insurance policy is a contract between an individual and an insurance company. The individual pays premiums to the insurance company, and in exchange, the company promises to pay a death benefit to the individual's beneficiaries upon their death. The death benefit is typically tax-free to the beneficiaries and can be used to pay off debts, cover funeral expenses, and provide income for the surviving family members.

In Jane's case, her advisor suggested that she consider purchasing a **whole life insurance policy**. Whole life insurance is a type of permanent life insurance that offers both a death benefit and a cash value component. The cash value grows tax-free over time and can be accessed by the policyholder through loans or withdrawals. Additionally, whole life insurance policies typically have level premiums, which means that the premium payments remain the same throughout the life of the policy.

Jane was hesitant about the idea of paying premiums for a life insurance policy at her age, but her advisor explained that the premiums would be relatively small compared to the potential tax savings for her estate. The death benefit of the policy would also be a way for her to leave a legacy for her children and grandchildren.

Jane decided to move forward with purchasing a whole life insurance policy. She chose a policy with a death benefit of $2 million and a premium of $30,000 per year. The policy would be paid for out of her estate, and the death benefit would be distributed tax-free to her beneficiaries upon her death.

Over the years, Jane watched as the cash value of her policy grew steadily. She was able to access the cash value to help cover unexpected expenses, such as medical bills and home repairs. She also used the policy as a way to transfer wealth to her children and grandchildren while she was still alive. She took out policy loans to make gifts to her family members, which allowed her to avoid gift taxes.

When Jane passed away at the age of 85, her children and grandchildren were grateful for the life insurance policy she had purchased. The death benefit helped to pay off her outstanding debts and provide income for her surviving family members. The policy also helped to preserve her fortune for her beneficiaries, who received the death benefit tax-free.

Joseph Kohen Helps His Grandchildren

Joseph Kohen was a retired grandfather who was always close to his grandchildren. He wanted to ensure that they were financially secure even after he was gone. So he decided to look into purchasing a life insurance policy that might help him provide for their financial future.

After doing some research, Joseph decided to purchase a whole life insurance policy. This type of policy provided a guaranteed death benefit to his beneficiaries, which in this case would be his grandchildren. Additionally, it had a cash value component that can grow over time and can be accessed by the policy owner, Joseph, during his lifetime if needed.

Joseph decides to purchase a policy with a death benefit of $250,000. He knew that this amount would be enough to provide for his grandchildren's future needs, such as college tuition or a down payment on a house.

Joseph's policy also had a cash value component that can be accessed during his lifetime. He decided to use this feature to help pay for his grandchildren's education expenses while he was still alive. You see, Joseph could borrow against the cash value of his policy and use the funds to pay for his grandchildren's education: he knew that he will have to pay back the loan with interest, but he saw this as a way to help his grandchildren get the education they need without having to worry about how to pay for it.

In addition to providing for his grandchildren's education, Joseph also wanted to leave them with a financial legacy. He decided to name his grandchildren as the beneficiaries of his policy. This means that when he passes away, the death benefit will go directly to them, bypassing the probate process and any potential taxes.

Joseph knows that his grandchildren will likely face many financial challenges in their lives, such as unexpected medical expenses or job loss. So he wanted to make sure that they have a financial safety net in place.

With his whole life insurance policy, Joseph feels confident that he has taken the necessary steps to provide for his grandchildren's financial future.

When Joseph eventually passes away, his grandchildren will be devastated. However, they will be grateful for the education and financial security that their grandfather has provided for them. With the death benefit from the policy, they are able to pay off any outstanding debts and have enough left over to invest in their own futures.

Understanding Exactly What Permanent Insurance Is: The Life Long and Long Life Option

Whole Life Insurance

Whole life insurance is a type of life insurance that can help protect you and your family in case something bad happens: whether it is death, or certain types of severe injuries, or sicknesses. It works by combining a death benefit with a savings account that can grow over time.

With whole life insurance, you pay a premium every month, and a portion of that premium goes towards the death benefit, which is the amount of money your family will receive if you pass away. The rest of the premium goes into a savings account that earns interest over time. This means that you can use some of the money you pay into your policy to save for things like your retirement or a down payment on a house.

One of the benefits of whole life insurance is that the savings account can earn interest at a fixed rate, meaning it stays the same. This can help you plan for the future and provide a stable source of savings.

Whole life insurance policies also offer the benefit of a guaranteed death benefit, which means that your family will receive a certain amount of money when you pass away, as long as you continue to pay your premiums.

Overall, whole life insurance is a way to help protect your loved ones financially, while also providing a way to save for the future. It's important to understand the costs and benefits of this type of policy before making a decision, and to work with a trusted insurance agent to make sure it's the right choice for you and your family.

Tax Deferred Growth
Similar to an IRA, your policy grows tax-deferred.

Tax-Advantaged Distributions
Similar to a ROTH IRA, you can pull money out of your policy without paying taxes.

No Additional Tax for Early Withdrawals
Unlike qualified accounts such as 401(k) and IRA's, you can access the policy cash values pre-59.5 without incurring taxes or penalties.

No Increased Tax Expenses
Unlike a 401(k) and Traditional IRA, you can access the policy cash values without increasing your Social Security tax or Medicare premiums.

Guaranteed Growth
Your policy grows based on the guarantees of the insurance carrier and can grow even more based on dividends.

Income Tax Free Death Benefit
Your beneficiary receives the death benefit income tax free.

Whole life insurance is a type of permanent life insurance that provides a guaranteed death benefit to beneficiaries upon the policyholder's death, as well as a cash value component that accumulates over time. Unlike term life insurance, which provides coverage for a specified period, whole life insurance provides coverage for the policyholder's entire life, as long as the policy premiums are paid.

Guaranteed Death Benefit

One of the primary features of whole life insurance is its **guaranteed death benefit**. The death benefit is the amount of money that is paid to the policy's beneficiaries upon the policyholder's death, and with whole life insurance, the death benefit is guaranteed, regardless of when the policyholder dies. This means that policyholders can have peace of mind knowing that their loved ones will receive a payout, no matter when they pass away.

Cash Value Component

Another key feature of whole life insurance is the **cash value component**. The cash value is the amount of money that accumulates in the policy over time, and it grows tax-deferred. Whole life insurance policies are typically designed to build cash value over time, and policyholders can access the cash value through policy loans or withdrawals. This means that policyholders can use the cash value to supplement their retirement income, pay for unexpected expenses, or fund their children's education.

Whole life insurance policies also typically come with a fixed premium that is guaranteed for the life of the policy. This means that policyholders can budget for their premiums and avoid unexpected rate increases, which can be a concern with other types of life insurance policies.

Different Types

There are different types of whole life insurance policies, including traditional whole life, universal life, and variable life. Traditional whole life insurance policies invest the policy premiums in the insurer's general account, where they earn interest. The insurer then deducts fees and expenses, and the remainder of the interest is credited to the policy's cash value.

Universal life insurance policies, on the other hand, provide policyholders with more flexibility when it comes to premium payments and death benefits. Policyholders can adjust the premium payments and death benefits over time, which allows them to customize their coverage to fit their changing needs.

Variable life insurance policies allow policyholders to invest the policy premiums in a variety of investment options, such as mutual funds. The cash value component of the policy can fluctuate based on the performance of the investments. This means that policyholders have the potential to earn higher returns than they would with traditional or universal whole life insurance policies, but they also face more investment risk.

When considering whole life insurance, it's important to weigh the costs and benefits. Whole life insurance premiums are typically higher than term life insurance premiums, and the policy's cash value may take several years to accumulate. However, the guaranteed death benefit and the ability to access the cash value can be attractive features for some policyholders.

Additionally, whole life insurance policies may be an attractive option for individuals who have long-term financial goals and want a reliable way to build wealth over time. Policyholders can use the cash value to supplement their retirement income, fund a child's education, or leave a legacy to their loved ones.

Overall, whole life insurance is a type of permanent life insurance that provides a guaranteed death benefit and a cash value component that accumulates over time. With a fixed premium, policyholders can budget for their coverage and avoid unexpected rate increases. However, it's important to carefully consider the costs and benefits of whole life insurance before making a decision, and to work with a financial professional to ensure that the policy meets the individual's unique financial goals and needs

Universal Life Insurance

Summary

Universal life insurance is a type of life insurance that can help protect you and your family in case something bad happens: not only death, but certain types of injuries and sicknesses too. It works by combining a savings account with a life insurance policy. This means that you can use some of the money you pay into your policy to save for things like your retirement, while still having a death benefit to help your family if you pass away.

Universal life insurance policies are flexible, which means you can change the amount you pay into your policy each month, as long as you pay a certain minimum amount. You can also adjust the amount of the death benefit if your needs change over time.

One of the benefits of universal life insurance is that the money in the savings account can earn interest over time. The interest rate can be fixed, meaning it stays the same, or it can be tied to a stock market index, which means it can go up or down depending on how the stock market does. However, it's important to understand that with a stock market index, there is also the risk that the interest rate can go down.

Overall, universal life insurance is a way to help protect your loved ones financially, while also providing a way to save for the future.

Payout

Universal Life benefits are paid when the insured dies and the beneficiary files a death claim with the insurance company. The default payout option is a lump sum check.

Flexible Premium
Your premium payments are customizable throughout the life of the policy. For example, you can lower the premiums or skip them altogether which would reduce your cash value or cause the policy to end sooner. You can also pay additional premiums to increase the cash value or be able to skip future premiums.

Cash Values
Universal Life is generally purchased to achieve a death benefit that lasts your whole life for the least amount of premium, not for cash values. Plan on having minimal cash values.

Income Tax Free Death Benefit
Your beneficiary receives the death benefit income tax free.

Universal life insurance (UL) is a type of permanent life insurance that provides a death benefit to beneficiaries upon the policyholder's death. Unlike term life insurance, which only covers the insured for a specified period, universal life insurance policies provide coverage for the insured's entire lifetime, as long as the policy premiums are paid.

One of the main features of universal life insurance is its flexibility. Policyholders can choose the amount of premium they pay and when they pay it. This allows them to adjust their coverage to their changing needs over time. For example, if a policyholder's financial situation changes, they can increase or decrease their premium payments, and the death benefit will adjust accordingly. This flexibility is attractive to many people because it allows them to customize their policy to fit their unique financial circumstances.

Another key feature of universal life insurance is the death benefit. The death benefit is the amount of money that is paid to the policy's beneficiaries upon the insured's death. With universal life insurance, the death benefit can be adjusted over time to meet the policyholder's changing needs. For example, if the policyholder has children who are no longer dependents, they may want to reduce the death benefit to save on premiums. Alternatively, if the policyholder has additional dependents or liabilities, they can increase the death benefit to ensure their beneficiaries are adequately protected.

One important consideration when purchasing universal life insurance is the cost. Universal life insurance premiums are typically higher than term life insurance premiums, but they provide lifelong coverage and build cash value. Additionally, because policyholders have the flexibility to adjust their premiums, the cost can vary over time. It's important for policyholders to review their policy regularly to ensure they are comfortable with the premiums and the coverage.

Overall, universal life insurance is a flexible and customizable type of permanent life insurance that can provide lifelong coverage and build cash value. With the ability to adjust premiums and death benefits, policyholders can tailor their coverage to fit their unique financial situation. However, it's important to carefully consider the cost and review the policy regularly to ensure it continues to meet the policyholder's needs over time.

There are two types of universal life insurance policies: traditional and indexed.

Traditional UL

Traditional UL policies invest the policy premiums in the insurer's general account, where they earn interest. The insurer then deducts fees and expenses, and the remainder of the interest is credited to the policy's cash value. The cash value is the amount of money that accumulates in the policy over time and can be used to pay future premiums or withdrawn by the policyholder.

Indexed UL

Indexed UL policies, on the other hand, invest the policy premiums in an index such as the S&P 500. The policyholder is credited with a portion of the index's gains, up to a cap rate set by the insurer, and protected from its losses. This allows policyholders to potentially earn a higher return on their investment than they would with a traditional UL policy.

Guaranteed Universal Life

Guaranteed Universal Life (GUL) is a type of life insurance that offers a guaranteed death benefit to your loved ones when you pass away. It's similar to other types of life insurance, but it has some unique features that make it different.

With GUL, you pay a premium every month, and the policy offers a fixed death benefit that is guaranteed as long as you continue to pay your premiums. Unlike some other types of life insurance, GUL typically does not have a savings component or cash value accumulation. This means that you pay only for the cost of insurance, which can be lower than other types of permanent life insurance policies.

GUL is a good option for people who want the peace of mind of knowing that their loved ones will be taken care of financially, without having to pay higher premiums for a policy that has a savings component. It's also a good option for people who are looking for a way to supplement their retirement income or to leave a legacy for their loved ones.

It's important to note that GUL premiums may increase over time if the policy was not purchased with the right guarantees, so it's important to work with a trusted insurance agent to ensure that you understand the policy terms and guarantees before purchasing. Overall, GUL can be a valuable option for people looking for a simple, affordable way to protect their loved ones financially.

Income Tax Free Payout

Guaranteed Universal Life (GUL) benefits are paid when the insured dies and the beneficiary files a death claim with the insurance company. The default payout option is a lump sum check. Your beneficiary receives the death benefit income tax free.

Coverage for a set number of years
Coverage is guaranteed to last to a specific age. Unlike term insurance, GUL can last for your entire life. GUL is sometimes referred to as "Term for Life"

Cash Values
GUL is generally purchased to achieve a death benefit that lasts your whole life for the least amount of premium, not for cash values. Plan on having minimum to no cash values.

Guaranteed universal life insurance (GUL) is a type of permanent life insurance policy that provides a death benefit and guarantees a fixed premium payment for the policyholder's entire life. It is similar to traditional universal life insurance in that it offers more flexibility than whole life insurance, but it is also different in that it is designed to be less expensive and provide fewer investment options.

Unlike traditional universal life insurance, GUL policies are not designed to accumulate cash value. Instead, the focus is on providing a death benefit that is guaranteed to pay out as long as the policy premiums are paid. The premium payment is fixed and remains the same throughout the policy's lifetime, which allows policyholders to budget for the cost of the policy and avoid unexpected rate increases.

One of the main advantages of GUL is that it offers a level of predictability and stability that other types of life insurance policies may not. Since the premium payment is fixed, policyholders can be confident that they will be able to afford the cost of the policy for the duration of their life. Additionally, since the death benefit is guaranteed, policyholders can have peace of mind knowing that their beneficiaries will receive a payout upon their death.

GUL policies are typically less expensive than traditional universal life insurance policies, making them an attractive option for individuals who want permanent life insurance coverage but may not be able to afford the higher premiums associated with other types of permanent life insurance. Additionally, since GUL policies do not have a cash value component, policyholders do not have to worry about the performance of the policy's investments.

GUL policies may be particularly well-suited for individuals who are looking for long-term life insurance coverage to protect their families or provide for estate planning purposes. Since GUL policies offer a guaranteed death benefit, they can be used to provide a source of income for beneficiaries or to pay estate taxes upon the policyholder's death.

However, it's important to note that GUL policies are not without their limitations. Unlike traditional universal life insurance policies, GUL policies typically do not offer the same level of flexibility when it comes to premium payments or death benefits. Additionally, since there is no cash value component, policyholders cannot use the policy as an investment vehicle to accumulate wealth over time.

It's also important to carefully consider the terms of the policy before purchasing a GUL policy. Some policies may have restrictions on the death benefit payout or the premium payment structure, so it's important to work with a financial professional to ensure that the policy meets the policyholder's unique needs and financial goals.

In summary, GUL is a type of permanent life insurance policy that provides a guaranteed death benefit and a fixed premium payment for the policyholder's entire life. While it may be less expensive than other types of permanent life insurance, it also offers fewer investment options and less flexibility when it comes to premium payments and death benefits. However, it can be an attractive option for individuals who are looking for long-term life insurance coverage to protect their families or provide for estate planning purposes. As with any type of life insurance, it's important to carefully consider the costs and benefits of GUL before making a decision and to work with a financial professional to ensure that the policy meets the individual's unique needs and goals.

Protection Indexed Universal Life

Protection Indexed Universal Life (IUL) is similar to other types of life insurance, but it has some unique features that make it different.

With Protection IUL, you pay a premium every month, and a portion of that premium goes towards a death benefit, which is the amount of money your loved ones will receive if you pass away. The rest of the premium goes towards a savings account that earns interest based on the performance of an index, such as the S&P 500. This means that your savings can potentially grow over time, but there is also a risk that the interest rate can go down.

One of the benefits of Protection IUL is that it offers flexibility in terms of how much you pay and how much coverage you have. You can adjust your premium payments or death benefit if your needs change over time. Protection IUL also offers tax benefits, as the cash value growth is tax-deferred.

Overall, Protection IUL is a way to help protect your loved ones financially, while also providing a way to save for the future. It's important to understand the costs and benefits of this type of policy before making a decision, and to work with a trusted insurance agent to make sure it's the right choice for you and your family

Tax Deferred Growth

Similar to an IRA, your policy grows tax-deferred.

Tax-Advantaged Distributions

Similar to a ROTH IRA, you can pull money out of your policy without paying taxes.

No Additional Tax for Early Withdrawals

Unlike qualified accounts such as 401(k) and IRA's, you can access the policy cash values pre-59.5 without incurring taxes or penalties.

No Increased Tax Expenses

Unlike a 401(k) and Traditional IRA, you can access the policy cash values without increasing your Social Security tax or Medicare premiums.

Upside Potential with Downside Protection

Your policy grows based on the performance of the S&P 500, subject to a floor and a cap.

Income Tax Free Death Benefit

Your beneficiary receives the death benefit income tax free.

Protection Indexed Universal Life (IUL) insurance is a type of permanent life insurance policy that provides both death benefit protection and the potential for cash value accumulation. The IUL abbreviation stands for Indexed Universal Life, which refers to the way the policy's cash value is tied to the performance of a stock market index.

Unlike traditional universal life insurance policies, which offer a fixed or variable interest rate on the policy's cash value, IUL policies offer policyholders the ability to earn interest based on the performance of a stock market index. Policyholders can choose from a variety of different indexes, such as the S&P 500 or the NASDAQ 100, and their cash value will be credited with interest based on the performance of that index, subject to caps and floors set by the insurance company.

One of the main advantages of IUL policies is the potential for cash value accumulation. As the policy's cash value grows over time, policyholders can use it to pay for premiums or take out loans against the policy. Additionally, since the policy's cash value is tied to the performance of a stock market index, policyholders have the potential to earn higher returns on their investment than they would with a traditional universal life insurance policy.

Another advantage of IUL policies is the flexibility they offer when it comes to premium payments. Policyholders can choose to pay premiums on a schedule that works best for their financial situation, whether that be annually, semi-annually, or monthly. Additionally, some policies may offer the option to skip premium payments or adjust the premium amount over time.

IUL policies can be particularly well-suited for individuals who are looking for long-term life insurance coverage and want to use the policy's cash value component as an investment vehicle. The potential for cash value accumulation can provide a source of tax-advantaged savings for retirement or other financial goals, and policyholders can access the cash value through loans or withdrawals as needed.

However, it's important to carefully consider the risks and limitations of IUL policies before making a decision. One risk is that the policy's cash value may not grow as quickly as expected or may even decrease in value if the stock market index performs poorly. Additionally, some policies may have caps and floors that limit the amount of interest credited to the cash value, which can impact the policy's overall performance.

It's also important to understand that IUL policies typically come with higher fees and expenses than other types of life insurance policies. Since the policy's cash value is tied to the performance of a stock market index, insurance companies may charge additional fees to cover the costs of managing the policy's investments.

Finally, it's important to understand the policy's death benefit structure and how it may impact the policyholder's beneficiaries. While IUL policies offer the potential for cash value accumulation, the primary purpose of the policy is still to provide a death benefit to the policyholder's beneficiaries. If the policy's cash value is used to pay for premiums or taken out in loans, it may impact the death benefit payout.

In summary, Protection IUL is a type of permanent life insurance policy that offers both death benefit protection and the potential for cash value accumulation based on the performance of a stock market index. While it may offer more flexibility and investment potential than other types of permanent life insurance, it also comes with higher fees and expenses and carries the risk of lower returns if the stock market index underperforms. As with any type of life insurance, it's important to carefully consider the costs and benefits of Protection IUL before making a decision and to work with a financial professional to ensure that the policy meets the individual's unique needs and financial goals.

Accumulation Indexed Universal Life

Accumulation Indexed Universal Life (IUL) is a type of life insurance that can help you save money for the future while also providing a death benefit for your loved ones. It's similar to other types of life insurance, but it has some unique features that make it different.

With Accumulation IUL, you pay a premium every month, and a portion of that premium goes towards a death benefit for your loved ones. The rest of the premium goes towards a savings account that earns interest based on the performance of an index, such as the S&P 500. This means that your savings can potentially grow over time, but there is also a risk that the interest rate can go down.

One of the benefits of Accumulation IUL is that it offers flexibility in terms of how much you pay and how much coverage you have. You can adjust your premium payments or death benefit if your needs change over time. Accumulation IUL also offers tax benefits, as the cash value growth is tax-deferred.

Overall, Accumulation IUL is a way to help protect your loved ones financially, while also providing a way to save for the future. It's important to understand the costs and benefits of this type of policy before making a decision, and to work with a trusted insurance agent to make sure it's the right choice for you and your family.

Tax Deferred Cash Value Growth Potential
Any cash value growth is tax-deferred.

Tax-Advantaged Cash Value Distributions

Policy loans and withdrawals are generally tax-free. Policy loans and withdrawals reduce the policy's cash value and death benefit and may result in a taxable event. Withdrawals up to the basis paid into the contract and loans thereafter will not create an immediate taxable event, but substantial tax ramifications could result upon contract lapse or surrender. Surrender charges may reduce the policy's cash value in early years.

Not Subject to Access Restrictions Like Retirement Accounts

Unlike retirement accounts, there is no minimum age to access policy values without tax penalties. The ability to take policy loans or withdrawals will depend on the amount accumulated and is not guaranteed. Excessive loans or withdrawals could result in a lapse of the policy which may result in tax ramifications.

icy Loans and Withdrawals Are Generally Not Recognized as Income

Proceeds from policy loans and withdrawals currently don't impact income calculations for Social Security, Medicare or Expected Family Contribution (Federal Financial Aid for College).

Upside Potential with Downside Protection

Interest is credited based in part on the performance of a market index, such as the S&P 500, subject to a floor and cap. The cap is the highest amount of the index's performance that will be credited as interest. The 0% "floor" ensures that during crediting periods where the index is negative, that no less than 0% interest is credited to the index strategy. However, monthly deductions continue to be taken from the cash value, including a monthly policy fee, monthly expense charge, cost of insurance charge, and applicable rider charges, regardless of interest crediting.

Income Tax Free Death Benefit

Your beneficiary receives the death benefit income tax free (Internal Revenue Code § 101(a)(1). There are some exceptions to this rule.)

Accumulation Indexed Universal Life (AIUL) insurance is a type of permanent life insurance policy that offers both death benefit protection and the potential for cash value accumulation based on the performance of a stock market index. AIUL policies are designed to provide policyholders with a flexible and tax-efficient way to save for long-term financial goals, such as retirement or college expenses.

Like other types of indexed universal life (IUL) insurance, AIUL policies offer the potential for cash value accumulation based on the performance of a stock market index, such as the S&P 500 or the NASDAQ 100. However, AIUL policies typically offer a more aggressive investment strategy that aims to maximize the policy's cash value growth potential.

One of the primary advantages of AIUL policies is the flexibility they offer in terms of premium payments. Policyholders can choose to pay premiums on a schedule that works best for their financial situation, whether that be annually, semi-annually, or monthly. Additionally, some policies may offer the option to skip premium payments or adjust the premium amount over time.

AIUL policies also offer a variety of different investment options that allow policyholders to customize their policy's investment strategy to match their risk tolerance and financial goals. For example, some policies may offer a choice of different stock market indexes or investment funds, while others may allow policyholders to invest in a mix of stocks, bonds, and other investment vehicles.

Another advantage of AIUL policies is the potential for tax-advantaged savings. Since the policy's cash value grows tax-deferred, policyholders can benefit from the compounding effect of their investment earnings over time. Additionally, if the policyholder chooses to take out loans against the policy's cash value, those loans may be tax-free as long as they are repaid.

However, it's important to carefully consider the risks and limitations of AIUL policies before making a decision. One risk is that the policy's cash value may not grow as quickly as expected or may even decrease in value if the stock market index performs poorly. Additionally, some policies may have caps and floors that limit the amount of interest credited to the cash value, which can impact the policy's overall performance.

It's also important to understand the policy's death benefit structure and how it may impact the policyholder's beneficiaries. While AIUL policies offer the potential for cash value accumulation, the primary purpose of the policy is still to provide a death benefit to the policyholder's beneficiaries. If the policy's cash value is used to pay for premiums or taken out in loans, it may impact the death benefit payout.

Finally, it's important to work with a financial professional who can help guide you through the complex investment and tax considerations of AIUL policies. Since these policies are designed to provide both insurance and investment benefits, it's important to have a comprehensive understanding of how the policy works and how it fits into your overall financial plan.

In summary, Accumulation Indexed Universal Life (AIUL) insurance is a type of permanent life insurance policy that offers both death benefit protection and the potential for cash value accumulation based on the performance of a stock market index. While it may offer more flexibility and investment potential than other types of permanent life insurance, it also comes with higher fees and expenses and carries the risk of lower returns if the stock market index underperforms. As with any type of life insurance, it's important to carefully consider the costs and benefits of AIUL before making a decision and to work with a financial professional to ensure that the policy meets the individual's unique needs and financial goals.

Understanding Exactly What Term Insurance Is: the Temporary Option

Several Kinds of Term Insurance

Unlike permanent life insurance policies, such as whole life insurance, term life insurance does not have a savings component or cash value accumulation. This means that the premiums you pay only cover the cost of insurance, and do not accumulate any cash value over time.

Term life insurance is a type of insurance that provides coverage for a specific period of time, known as the term. This could be for 1 year, 5 years, 10 years, or even 30 years. If you pass away during the term of your policy, your beneficiaries will receive a payout, called a death benefit, from the insurance company.

Term life insurance is a good option for people who want affordable coverage for a specific period of time. It's also a good option for people who have financial obligations, such as a mortgage or children's education, that will end after a certain number of years.

Overall, term life insurance provides peace of mind for you and your loved ones by ensuring that they are financially protected if something unexpected were to happen to you during the term of the policy

There are several types of term life insurance policies, including level term, decreasing term, and increasing term.

Level Term

Level term policies are the most common type of term life insurance. With this type of policy, the death benefit and premium remain level throughout the term of the policy. This means that you pay the same premium each year and your beneficiaries will receive the same payout if you pass away during the term of the policy. Level term policies are a good option for people who want a fixed premium and a guaranteed payout.

Decreasing Term

Decreasing term policies are another type of term life insurance. With this type of policy, the death benefit decreases over time, typically at a set rate each year. This type of policy is often used to cover a specific debt, such as a mortgage, that decreases over time. Decreasing term policies have lower premiums than level term policies, but the death benefit decreases over time.

Increasing term policies are the least common type of term life insurance. With this type of policy, the death benefit increases over time, typically at a set rate each year. This type of policy is often used to cover the rising cost of inflation or to provide additional coverage as you age. Increasing term policies have higher premiums than level term policies, but the death benefit increases over time.

Term life insurance is a good option for people who want affordable coverage for a specific period of time. It's also a good option for people who have financial obligations, such as a mortgage or children's education, that will end after a certain number of years.

When deciding how much term life insurance coverage you need, it's important to consider your current and future financial obligations, such as mortgage payments, college tuition, and other debts. You should also consider your income and how much your family would need to maintain their standard of living if you were no longer around to provide for them.

Term life insurance policies typically have lower premiums than permanent life insurance policies, which can make them more affordable for people on a budget. However, it's important to remember that term life insurance only provides coverage for a specific period of time, and once the term ends, you will no longer have coverage unless you renew the policy or purchase a new one

Typical Riders

What If You Don't Die? You May Want A Return of Premium Rider

A return of premium (ROP) rider is an optional feature that can be added to a term life insurance policy. Essentially, it offers a way for policyholders to recoup the premiums they've paid into the policy if they outlive the term of the policy.

With a standard term life insurance policy, if the policyholder dies during the term of the policy, the death benefit is paid out to the beneficiaries. However, if the policyholder outlives the term of the policy, the coverage ends and there is no payout or refund of premiums paid.

With an ROP rider, the insurance company will refund the premiums paid by the policyholder if they outlive the term of the policy. Essentially, the policyholder will receive a return of the premiums they paid in, tax-free, at the end of the term.

While an ROP rider may sound like a good deal, it typically comes at a higher premium cost than a standard term life insurance policy. This is because the insurance company is taking on more risk by offering the possibility of a premium refund. Additionally, some ROP riders may have restrictions or limitations on when the policyholder can receive the refund, such as only after a certain number of years have passed or if the policy is kept in force until the end of the term.

When considering an ROP rider, it's important to weigh the cost against the potential benefits. If the policyholder outlives the term of the policy, they may be able to receive a refund of premiums paid, which could be a significant sum of money.

However, if the policyholder passes away during the term of the policy, the higher premium paid for the ROP rider may not be worth it.

It's also important to note that an ROP rider is only available on term life insurance policies. It cannot be added to other types of life insurance, such as whole life or universal life insurance policies.

Overall, an ROP rider is a way for policyholders to receive a refund of premiums paid if they outlive the term of their policy. While it may come at a higher cost, it can provide peace of mind and financial protection for those who want to ensure that their premiums are not "wasted" if they outlive the policy. It's important to carefully consider the cost and potential benefits of an ROP rider before adding it to a term life insurance policy.

For Injuries, Sickness, Disease and Disability You May Want Living Benefits

A living benefits rider is an optional feature that can be added to a term life insurance policy. It allows the policyholder to access a portion of their death benefit while they are still alive if they are diagnosed with a terminal illness or other qualifying medical condition.

Essentially, a living benefits rider provides financial support to policyholders who are facing a serious illness. If the policyholder is diagnosed with a terminal illness and is expected to pass away within a certain period of time, typically two years, they can access a portion of their death benefit to help cover medical expenses, pay bills, or provide for their family.

Unlike a traditional life insurance policy, which only pays out a death benefit to beneficiaries after the policyholder passes away, a living benefits rider allows policyholders to access some of that money while they are still alive. This can be especially helpful for individuals who may not have other financial resources to cover medical expenses or other costs associated with a serious illness.

It's important to note that accessing the death benefit through a living benefits rider will reduce the overall amount of money that the beneficiaries will receive when the policyholder passes away. However, this can be a worthwhile tradeoff if it means that the policyholder is able to receive much-needed financial support during a difficult time.

In order to qualify for a living benefits rider, the policyholder must meet certain medical criteria. Typically, this means that they must have a terminal illness or a condition that is expected to significantly impact their life expectancy. The specific requirements for a living benefits rider may vary depending on the insurance company and the policy.

Adding a living benefits rider to a term life insurance policy can provide additional financial security and peace of mind for policyholders and their families. It's important to carefully consider the cost and potential benefits of a living benefits rider before adding it to a policy. Additionally, it's important to work with a reputable insurance company and carefully review the terms and conditions of the rider to ensure that it meets your specific needs and circumstances.

Conversion

A conversion rider is a special feature that can be added to a term life insurance policy. This rider allows the policyholder to convert their term policy to a permanent life insurance policy, such as whole life insurance, without having to go through a medical exam or underwriting process again.

When you purchase a term life insurance policy, it is only good for a certain amount of time, called the term. If you pass away during this term, your beneficiaries will receive a death benefit payout. However, if the term ends and you are still alive, your coverage will expire and you will not receive any payout.

A conversion rider allows you to avoid losing your coverage by converting your term policy to a permanent life insurance policy. Permanent life insurance policies last for the entire lifetime of the policyholder, as long as the premiums are paid, and they also have a cash value component that can grow over time.

With a conversion rider, you can convert your term policy to a permanent policy without having to go through a medical exam or underwriting process again. This can be especially beneficial if your health has declined since you first purchased your term policy, as you may not be able to qualify for a new policy at the same rates.

And, for those unfamiliar with the aging process: as people grow older, they *will certainly* develop health conditions that will result in higher premiums. Or make it impossible to get coverage.

It is important to note that there are usually time limits for when you can exercise your conversion rider. For example, you may only have the option to convert your policy during the first 10 years of the term, or before a certain age. It is important to review your policy documents and understand the specific rules and limitations of your conversion rider.

Overall, a conversion rider can be a valuable addition to a term life insurance policy, as it allows you to maintain coverage and potentially convert to a permanent policy without having to go through additional medical exams or underwriting.

Long Term Care

A long term care rider is a type of insurance coverage that can be added to a life insurance policy to help cover the cost of long term care services if you become chronically ill or disabled. This rider can help you pay for expenses associated with care in a nursing home, assisted living facility, or even in your own home.

The long term care rider works by providing a monthly benefit to help cover the cost of care. This benefit is typically based on a percentage of the death benefit of the policy, and can range from 1% to 4% per month. For example, if the death benefit of your life insurance policy is $100,000 and your long term care rider provides a monthly benefit of 2%, you would receive $2,000 per month to help cover the cost of care.

One of the benefits of a long term care rider is that it can help you maintain your independence and quality of life. If you become chronically ill or disabled and require long term care, you may need assistance with daily activities such as bathing, dressing, and eating. This can be challenging both physically and emotionally, and having the financial resources to pay for care can help you maintain your dignity and independence.

Another benefit of a long term care rider is that it can help protect your assets. Long term care can be expensive, and if you do not have the financial resources to pay for care, you may need to rely on government programs such as Medicaid. However, Medicaid has strict eligibility requirements, and you may need to spend down your assets in order to qualify. With a long term care rider, you can help protect your assets and ensure that they are available to pass on to your loved ones.

It's important to note that there are some limitations to a long term care rider. For example, there may be a waiting period before benefits are paid, typically ranging from 30 to 90 days. In addition, there may be a maximum benefit period, which is the length of time that benefits will be paid. This can range from one to five years or longer, depending on the policy.

There may also be restrictions on the types of care that are covered. For example, some policies may only cover care in a nursing home or assisted living facility, while others may also cover home care. It's important to read the policy carefully and understand the terms and conditions of the rider.

How Much Coverage Do You Need? Making Sure You Are Not Overinsured or Underinsured

Estimating the amount of life insurance coverage needed can be a difficult decision for families to make, because it is easy to slip into the thought that you are estimating the value of a loved one's life. Of course you cannot do that - but what you can do is estimate how much money it would cost your family to care for that loved one if they become disabled, and if they were no longer able to help around the house or earn income.

Step 1: Calculate your current expenses

The first step in estimating life insurance coverage is to calculate your current expenses. This includes things like your mortgage or rent payment, utilities, groceries, car payments, insurance, and any other bills or expenses that you pay on a regular basis. Make sure to take into account any future expenses, such as college tuition or retirement savings.

Step 2: Consider future expenses

In addition to current expenses, it's important to consider future expenses as well. This could include things like college tuition for your children, major home repairs or renovations, and retirement savings. These expenses can be difficult to estimate, but it's important to try and account for them as accurately as possible.

It is important here to include potential costs of grief: whether there is disability or death, you will likely require time and money to grieve, and this means time from work, as well as psychological counseling.

Step 3: Calculate costs of home improvements to make the house accessible

The next step is to consider what your home might need if the loved one becomes disabled: would you need accessibility improvements for stairs? Bathroom remodels? Wider doorways? Would you need a long term caregiver?

Step 4: Determine how long your family will need financial support

Once you have a clear picture of your current and future expenses, it's important to determine how long your family will need this sort of financial support if something were to happen to the loved one. When children are grown, the household's expenses will be reduced. But costs will increase in retirement as well if the household did not get the chance to save for it because of lost income.

Step 5: Calculate the total amount needed

Once you have a clear idea of your expenses, income, and how long your family will need financial support, you can calculate the total amount of life insurance coverage that may be needed. This can be done by adding up all these costs.

It's important to note that estimating life insurance coverage can be a complex process, and it may be helpful to consult with a financial advisor or insurance professional to help ensure that you have a clear understanding of your options and the potential costs and benefits of each.

Conclusion: Everyone Can Use Life Insurance While Alive

Even Confirmed Bachelors and Bachelorettes can Use Life Insurance While They Are Alive

As a confirmed bachelor or bachelorette with no beneficiaries or heirs, it may seem like life insurance is unnecessary. However, whole life insurance can provide several benefits for individuals in this situation while they are still alive.

As an Investment

One of the primary benefits of whole life insurance is its cash value accumulation feature. When you purchase a whole life insurance policy, a portion of your premium payments goes towards building up the policy's cash value. This cash value is invested by the insurance company and grows over time with interest. As a policyholder, you can access this cash value through policy loans or withdrawals.

Tax Advantaged Emergency and Retirement Funding

For confirmed bachelors and bachelorettes, this cash value can serve as a valuable source of emergency funds or retirement income. Unlike other savings accounts, the cash value of a whole life insurance policy is protected from creditors and is not considered a taxable asset. This means that the money is available to you tax-free, even if you withdraw it before the age of 59 and a half.

Assisted Living (even at your own home!) and Nursing Homes When You're Old

In addition to the guaranteed death benefit, whole life insurance policies also offer the option of adding riders. Riders are additional benefits that can be added to your policy for an additional premium. One popular rider for confirmed bachelors and bachelorettes is the long-term care rider.

The long-term care rider provides benefits for individuals who require assistance with daily living activities, such as bathing, dressing, or eating. If you were to require long-term care services in the future, the long-term care rider can provide you with financial support to help cover these costs.

Another rider that may be beneficial for confirmed bachelors and bachelorettes is the disability income rider. This rider provides a monthly income in the event that you become disabled and are unable to work. This can provide a valuable source of income for individuals who do not have any other means of financial support.

Self Sufficient to the End

Another benefit of whole life insurance for confirmed bachelors and bachelorettes is the guaranteed death benefit. While you may not have any heirs or beneficiaries, it is still important to plan for the unexpected. If you were to pass away unexpectedly, your loved ones would be responsible for your final expenses. This can include funeral costs, outstanding debts, and any other expenses that arise as a result of your passing.

By purchasing a whole life insurance policy, you can ensure that these expenses are taken care of without burdening your loved ones. The death benefit of a whole life insurance policy is guaranteed, meaning that your loved ones will receive a set amount of money upon your passing. This can provide peace of mind for both you and your loved ones, knowing that your final expenses are taken care of.

Legacy

Lastly, whole life insurance can also serve as a legacy: even if you do not have children, by gifting the death benefit to your favorite charity or cause, or creating scholarships, or building clinics, shelters, schools, or doing other public good, you can establish a legacy for yourself that will stand the test of time, and help create a better world to come.

Babies and Children Too

When a baby is born, parents often have a lot of expenses to consider, such as medical bills, child care costs, and other expenses related to raising a child. One expense that may not immediately come to mind is purchasing an insurance policy for the newborn child. However, there are several reasons why parents may want to consider purchasing life insurance for their new baby.

Death or Disability of a Child

First and foremost, purchasing a life insurance policy for a newborn child can provide financial protection in the event of an unexpected tragedy, whether that is the death of the child, or their child becoming disabled. While no parent wants to think about the possibility of losing a child or of a terrible injury like that, the reality is that accidents and illnesses can happen at any time.

If a child becomes disabled, the costs of home modifications to make the house handicapped accessible, or for longterm caregiving assistance may be burdensome. And If the worst does happen and a child passes away, a life insurance policy can help cover the cost of funeral expenses and provide financial support to the family during a difficult time when they would likely prefer to take time from working to grieve.

However, this death is not a typical outcome for childhood. Most children will survive, and without disability, and it is not reasonable to worry overmuch about that sort of tragedy.

For When They Are All Grownup: Financial Independence

The best benefit of purchasing life insurance for a newborn child is that it can help secure their financial future. Depending on the type of policy purchased, a life insurance policy can build cash value over time, which can be used to help pay for college, provide a down payment on a first home, or serve as a source of retirement income. By purchasing a policy at a young age, parents can help ensure that their child has a financial safety net in place as they grow older.

Purchasing life insurance for a newborn child can be a relatively low-cost way to provide long-term financial protection.

Because children are generally considered low-risk from an insurance perspective, premiums for a child's life insurance policy may be lower than those for an adult. This means that parents can purchase a policy for their child at a relatively low cost and potentially lock in low premiums for the life of the policy.

Of course, every family's circumstances are different, and purchasing life insurance for a newborn child may not be the right choice for every family. However, it's important for parents to consider all of their options and carefully weigh the potential benefits and costs of purchasing a policy. By doing so, they can make an informed decision that helps provide financial security and peace of mind for their family's future.

Don't Forget Life Insurance for the Parents

When a spouse dies or becomes disabled, it is an unspeakable tragedy. Especially when there are children involved.

If a parent were to pass away unexpectedly, a life insurance policy can help cover the costs associated with raising a child, such as child care, education, and other expenses. This can be particularly important for families that rely on a single income, as the loss of that income can be devastating: the surviving single parent may struggle to provide for their children. But even if the spouse is a stay at home parent, the surviving breadwinner may struggle as a single parent to provide for appropriate daycare, housekeeping and other domestic services their spouse formerly provided.

Yet there is also the emotional cost to consider as well: as a single parent of a house in grief, there will be a higher burden upon the surviving spouse to provide emotional support to the children, and a financial need to take time from work to be at home.

Purchasing a life insurance policy for parents can help ensure that their children are taken care of financially in the event of an unexpected tragedy.

Yet another benefit of purchasing life insurance for parents is that it can help pay off any outstanding debts or mortgages. If a parent passes away with outstanding debts, those debts can become a burden on the surviving family members. By purchasing a life insurance policy, parents can help ensure that their debts are paid off and their family is not left with a financial burden.

Life insurance can also help provide long-term financial security for a family in many ways. Depending on the type of policy purchased, a life insurance policy can build cash value over time, which can be used to help pay for college, provide a down payment on a first home, or serve as a source of retirement income. By purchasing a policy at a young age, parents can help ensure that their family has a financial safety net in place as they grow older.

But there is also the need to consider that a newly disabled spouse will likely require home modifications to make the home more handicapped accessible, or even costly at home care: with living benefits, life insurance can help with these costs too.

<u>Yes, You Do Need Life Insurance!</u>

Everyone needs life insurance. Especially if you are not planning on dying anytime soon. Especially if you plan on fending off death as long as possible. By the very fact you are reading this book, it is likely you already understand this to some degree. So don't delay any longer! It is a hard decision, and a tough subject to think about, and an even more difficult choice to make. But it is one that you'll feel much better about once you do.

You've done the hard part already...you'll find the application is the easy part. So don't delay, reach out to an insurance agent today and start writing your own happily ever after!